MASTER YOUR SPELLING

G. C. Davies, S. M. Dillon and T. D. Dillon

Illustrated by G. C. Davies

Basil Blackwell

How to use this book

1 Look hard at the words in the first box on the page.
2 Copy out the first word neatly in large letters.
3 Trace over the letters with your finger.
4 Say the word slowly and spell it aloud.
5 Close your eyes. Make a picture of the word in your mind.
6 'Write' the word on the table with your finger.
7 Cover the word and really write it.
8 If it is correct, write it in your word book. If it is not, learn it again until you know it. *Then* write it in your word book.
9 Do this for each word in each box or in each puzzle.
10 The 'Pause for Thought' exercises are for extra practice.
11 Your teacher should mark the five tests in the book.

© 1983 G.C. Davies, S.M. Dillon and T.D. Dillon
All rights reserved.
First published 1983 Reprinted 1984, 1985, 1987, 1988, 1989
Published by Basil Blackwell Ltd
108 Cowley Road
Oxford OX4 1JF
Typeset in Linotron Century Schoolbook by Oxford Publishing Services
Printed in Hong Kong by Wing King Tong Co. Ltd.
ISBN 0 631 91090 5

| voice | choice | soil | noisy |
| boiled | rejoice | moist | toilet |

Complete these sentences. Use the words in the box.

1 Christmas is a time to r_____.
2 Polly has a very good singing v____.
3 The party was far too n____.
4 Plants must be kept m____ in dry spells.
5 You have a c_____, pudding or mince pies.
6 Please can I go to the t_____?
7 He pushed the spade into the s___.
8 I'd like two b_____ eggs, please.

| carrying | marrying | applying |
| supplying | hurrying | ferrying |

Complete these sentences. Use the words in the box.

1 Karen is thinking of a_____ for that job.
2 At rush hour everyone is h_____ to work.
3 The farm is now s_____ eggs to the shops.
4 Wendy is m_____ Ian at St Luke's church.
5 The boat is f_____ us across the river.
6 Aunt Lil was c_____ a big bag.

Rule

On this page the rule is: when the sound is long **e** write **i** before **e** except after **c**.

ie
or
ei

> mischief   grief   niece   deceive
> believe   chief   shield   ceiling
> thieves   thief   belief   receive

A pair of letters is missing from each word.
Crack the code and write out the complete words.

1 bel _ _ f
2 misch _ _ f
3 sh _ _ ld
4 th _ _ f
5 dec _ _ ve
6 n _ _ ce

7 bel _ _ ve
8 ch _ _ f
9 rec _ _ ve
10 gr _ _ f
11 th _ _ ves
12 c _ _ ling

> mischief   handkerchief   receive
> relief   ceiling   thief

Complete these sentences. Use the words in the box.

1 I expect to r _ _ _ _ _ _ an answer tomorrow.
2 Dad painted the c _ _ _ _ _ _ .
3 To Mum's great r _ _ _ _ _ , her purse was found.
4 The th _ _ _ stole the jewels.
5 Get a clean h _ _ _ _ _ _ _ _ _ _ and blow your nose.
6 Wilfred is always getting into m _ _ _ _ _ _ _ .

 **Soft c sounds like s.**

soft **C** sounds like **S**

| cemetery centre cell centigrade |
| century certain cement citizen |

Complete these sentences. Use the words in the box.

1 Yes, I am quite sure, I am c _ _ _ _ _ _.

2 The middle is also called the c _ _ _ _ _.

3 Water boils at 100 degrees c _ _ _ _ _ _ _ _.

4 We need sand and c _ _ _ _ _ to mend the wall.

5 A Londoner is a c _ _ _ _ _ _ of London.

6 A prisoner lives in a prison c _ _ _.

7 People are buried in a c _ _ _ _ _ _ _.

8 One hundred years is a c _ _ _ _ _ _.

Complete these sentences. Each dash stands for a letter.
Choose the correct word from the triple boxes.

1 If you think I'm guilty show me the p _ _ _ _. **assorted**

truth   evidence   proof

2 The hot-air b _ _ _ _ _ _ soared into the sky.

airship   balloon   helicopter

3 The road was widened to p _ _ _ _ _ _ accidents.

prevent   allow   encourage

4 Mini-skirts were in f _ _ _ _ _ _ in the 1960s.

shops   fashion   boxes

Pause for Thought

pages 3 to 5

> choice tooth relief chief balloon
> field hoof century noisy carrying
> shield certain cemetery hurrying
> cell centigrade handkerchief voice

Complete these sentences. Use the words in the box.

1. Uncle sat down with a huge sigh of r_____.
2. Water freezes at nought degrees c_____.
3. Blow up another b_____ for the party.
4. Go to the dentist and get that t____ filled.
5. Be quiet and try to be less n____.
6. Sam went h_____ off down the road.
7. Jenny sings well, she has a lovely v_____.
8. Make c_____ that knife is sharp.
9. The warder slammed the c___ door shut.
10. Sitting Bull was c____ of the Sioux tribe.
11. I'm tired of c_____ this bag, you take it.
12. Queen Victoria reigned in the nineteenth c_____.
13. The playing f____ is too wet to play on.
14. The lame horse had a stone in its h___.
15. The old c_____ is full of broken gravestones.
16. You have a c_____ of boiled potatoes or chips.
17. Have you got a clean h_____?
18. The Viking carried a sword and s_____.

| interval | medal | total | signal |
| capital | dismal | central | oval |

Complete these sentences. Use the words in the box.

1 Private Walker was awarded a m _ _ _ _.
2 The shopping precinct is in a c _ _ _ _ _ _ position.
3 Paris is the c _ _ _ _ _ _ city of France.
4 There will be a short i _ _ _ _ _ _ _ during the concert.
5 An egg is o _ _ _ in shape.
6 The train stopped because the s _ _ _ _ _ was red.
7 It has been a wet and d _ _ _ _ _ day.
8 Add both columns and find the t _ _ _ _.

| oral | metal | marshal | local |
| mental | royal | mutual | fatal |

Crack this code and write the answers in your book.
Use the words in the box.

1 lahsram
2 latnem
3 lacol
4 lataf

5 latem
6 layor
7 laro
8 lautum

| material   aerial   trial   trivial burial   special   serial |  |

Complete these sentences. Use the words in the box.

1 The TV a_ _ _ _ _ has fallen off the roof.
2 Smith's t_ _ _ _ will be at the Crown Court.
3 A s_ _ _ _ _ _ train will run from Liverpool.
4 The b_ _ _ _ _ will be in St Mark's churchyard.
5 Jim will continue reading the s_ _ _ _ _ tomorrow.
6 The dress is made of a silky m_ _ _ _ _ _ _.
7 Don't get upset over such a t_ _ _ _ _ _ matter.

| dual   usual   punctual mutual   manual   annual |  |

Complete these sentences. Use the words in the box.

1 Cherry Lane is now a d_ _ _ carriageway.
2 Your birthday is an a_ _ _ _ _ event.
3 Cars have either an automatic or m_ _ _ _ _ _ gearbox.
4 Late again, you should try to be more p_ _ _ _ _ _ _.
5 The exchange was to their m_ _ _ _ _ advantage.
6 The man asked for his u_ _ _ _ tobacco.

listened   rustling   castle   fasten
glistened   fastened   listen   whistle

Complete these sentences. Use the words in the box.

1   Did you l _ _ _ _ _ to that concert on Radio One?
2   Joe is so fat he cannot f _ _ _ _ _ his belt.
3   Everyone l _ _ _ _ _ _ _ to the speaker in silence.
4   The referee blew his w _ _ _ _ _ _.
5   The leaves made a r _ _ _ _ _ _ _ sound.
6   We all f _ _ _ _ _ _ _ our seat belts.
7   The dewdrops g _ _ _ _ _ _ _ _ in the morning sun.
8   The baron lived in a grim c _ _ _ _ _.

beautiful   grateful   hopeful
pitiful   careful

*Work out the mixed up words. They all end in **ful**.*
Use the words in the box.

1   We are **lufetarg** for all your kindness.
2   The team manager is **lfphoeu** of winning.
3   Be **facreul** how you handle that vase.
4   The kitten gave a **ftipilu** cry.
5   Alice wore a **lftabeuiu** necklace.

Test 1

pages 3 to 9

Complete these sentences. Each dash stands for a letter.

1 Don't bother me with such t_____ matters.

2 What a r_____ to be home again!

3 Joe is c_____ this is the way to go.

4 Do you have p____ he is the thief?

5 Surrender or die, the c_____ is simple.

6 Wilfred behaved in his u____ silly way.

7 Madrid is the c_____ city of Spain.

8 Will you be a_____ for Smith's job?

9 Water boils at 100 degrees c_____.

10 Our driving school cars have d___ controls.

11 All passengers should f_____ their seat belts.

12 The concert will resume after the i_____.

13 Be quiet, you are all too n____.

14 It has been a b_____ day today.

15 Mandy was c_____ a doll in her arms.

16 The doctor l_____ carefully to Anne's story.

17 Lumps of plaster fell from the c_____.

18 They locked Tom in a prison c___.

19 Six aircraft gave an a_____ display.

20 That crocodile needs c_____ handling.

tyres shoulder type boulder mould typing moult typist

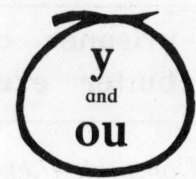

y
and
ou

Complete these sentences.
Use the words in the box.

1 Sarah is a t_____ in an office.
2 She learned to t___ at school.
3 Now she spends all day t_____ letters.
4 That car's t____ look threadbare.
5 Private Pop said the rifle hurt his s_____.
6 A huge b_____ rolled down the hillside.
7 The loaf is covered in green m____.
8 The budgie has started to m____ again.

favourite separate opposite deliberate desperate definite

ate
and
ite

Complete these sentences. Use the words in the box.

1 Phil made one last d_____ effort.
2 'Up' is the o_____ of 'down'.
3 Mike was quite d_____, he will not come.
4 That was a d_____ attempt to wreck the train.
5 Blue is my f_____ colour.
6 Our house has a s_____ dining room.

**prisoner consider remember supper
butter exercise better surrender**

Complete these sentences. Use the words in the box.

1 Take regular e _ _ _ _ _ _ _ to keep fit.

2 Jenny likes cocoa for s _ _ _ _ _ .

3 The escaped p _ _ _ _ _ _ _ stole a car.

4 You'll feel b _ _ _ _ _ after a rest.

5 You can't escape so why not s _ _ _ _ _ _ _ _ .

6 I hope you'll r _ _ _ _ _ _ _ Gran's birthday.

7 Put some b _ _ _ _ _ on your toast.

8 Try to c _ _ _ _ _ _ _ other people when you play.

**permit perhaps reserve
property pattern interesting**

Crack the code and write the words correctly.
*All the words have **er** in them.*
To help you: a = 1   b = 2   c = 3   and z = 26.

1 18 : 5 : 19 : 5 : 18 : 22 : 5

2 16 : 1 : 20 : 20 : 5 : 18 : 14

3 16 : 5 : 18 : 13 : 9 : 20

4 16 : 18 : 15 : 16 : 5 : 18 : 20 : 25

5 9 : 14 : 20 : 5 : 18 : 5 : 19 : 20 : 9 : 14 : 7

6 16 : 5 : 18 : 8 : 1 : 16 : 19

winner	dinner	support	common
correct	suppose	commit	
connect	suddenly	coffin	

Complete these words by adding the correct double consonant. Use the words in the box.

1	s	u	_	_	o	r	t	
2	c	o	_	_	i	t		
3	c	o	_	_	i	n		
4	w	i	_	_	e	r		
5	s	u	_	_	e	n	l	y
6	c	o	_	_	o	n		
7	d	i	_	_	e	r		
8	c	o	_	_	e	c	t	
9	s	u	_	_	o	s	e	
10	c	o	_	_	e	c	t	

mm
rr
nn
pp
dd
ff

| spanner | commence | command |
| effort | effect | shopping |

Complete these sentences. Use the words in the box.

1 On the c_____ "Charge!", attack the enemy.
2 Everyone must make an e_____ to be on time.
3 We like to do our s_____ at Tesbury's.
4 The sports will c_____ at two o'clock.
5 Punishing Wilfred has no e_____ at all.
6 I told Mike to be careful with his s_____.

consists	contented	continent	concert
conceal	concrete	confess	contact

con

Complete these sentences. Use the words in the box.

1 I must conf___ I forgot all about you.
2 We're going to the pop conc___ tonight.
3 The troops managed to conc___ the guns.
4 Wayne is quite cont_____ after that meal.
5 The mixture cons____ of nuts and raisins.
6 Sonia claims to have made cont___ with the aliens.
7 Africa is a very large cont_____.
8 Mr Green plans to lay a conc____ path.

convict	consume	conversation	control
convent	conduct	confident	conflict

Crack this code and write out the words correctly.
They all begin with **con.**
To help you: a = B   b = C   c = D   and z = A.

1 DPOGMJDU   5 DPOUSPM
2 DPOEVDU   6 DPOWFOU
3 DPOGJEFOU   7 DPOWJDU
4 DPOTVNF   8 DPOWFSTBUJPO

Pause for Thought

pages 11 to 14

dinner	type	favourite	correct	prisoner
permit	coffin	concert	consider	separate
contact	effort	control	exercise	commence
winner	mouldy	remember		

Complete these sentences. Use the words in the box.

1 The pop c _ _ _ _ _ _ is at the Roxy cinema.

2 This cheese is green and m _ _ _ _ _.

3 Turn to page 42 and do e _ _ _ _ _ _ _ 'B'.

4 The jury went out to c _ _ _ _ _ _ _ their verdict.

5 Police are hunting for an escaped p _ _ _ _ _ _ _.

6 You may c _ _ _ _ _ _ _ _ writing when I tell you to start.

7 Clive has a toy car with radio c _ _ _ _ _ _.

8 You have got every spelling c _ _ _ _ _ _.

9 Louise is the w _ _ _ _ _ of the skating contest.

10 We should r _ _ _ _ _ _ _ _ the fifth of November.

11 He was carried to the grave in an oak c _ _ _ _ _.

12 Sausages and chips for d _ _ _ _ _ today!

13 Come on, Mollie, make an e _ _ _ _ _ to get up.

14 Celia can t _ _ _ very fast on her typewriter.

15 Mr Beak had to s _ _ _ _ _ _ _ the fighting boys.

16 You need a p _ _ _ _ _ to go inside the building.

17 Try to c _ _ _ _ _ _ John and tell him the news.

18 The Zipps are my f _ _ _ _ _ _ _ _ group.

murmur purchase furnace figure burden furniture surface purpose	

Complete these sentences. Use the words in the box.

1 You have written a wrong f _ _ _ _ _ in that sum.

2 You did that on p _ _ _ _ _ _, not accidentally.

3 The table has a shiny s _ _ _ _ _ _.

4 The gold is heated in a f _ _ _ _ _ _.

5 I intend to p _ _ _ _ _ _ _ a new car.

6 Neddy's knees buckled under the heavy b _ _ _ _ _.

7 I could hear the m _ _ _ _ _ of bees working.

8 We need new f _ _ _ _ _ _ _ _ in this room.

assistance balance chance trance dance glance	

Complete these sentences. Use the words in the box.

1 Bob took a quick g _ _ _ _ _ in his driving mirror.

2 We have no c _ _ _ _ _ of beating Rovers.

3 Wake up, boy, you seem to be in a t _ _ _ _ _ today.

4 That tune makes me want to d _ _ _ _.

5 The police officer radioed a call for a _ _ _ _ _ _ _ _ _ _.

6 Great Marvo has a wonderful sense of b _ _ _ _ _ _.

estimate emigrate irrigate elevate donate calculate private navigate	

Complete these sentences. Use the words in the box.

1 This is p_____ property so get off.

2 We must dig trenches to i_____ the land.

3 It will be difficult to n_____ through the ice.

4 Chris says he will e_____ to America.

5 You must e_____ the distance then check it.

6 A computer is used to c_____ difficult operations.

7 Mr Gripple will d_____ £1000 to the fund.

8 The fire chief told them to e_____ the ladder.

scare declare aware beware share flare snare glare	

Use the letters in each triangle to complete the words.
All the words end in **are**. *Use the words in the box.*

1 s_____   4 d_____   7 f_____

2 b_____   5 g_____   8 s_____

3 s_____   6 a_____

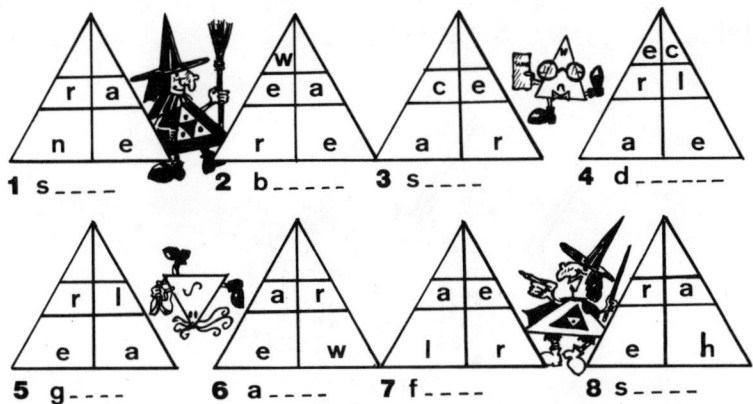

1 s____   2 b_____   3 s____   4 d_____

5 g____   6 a____   7 f____   8 s____

17

| computer compete comic complaint |  |
| combat compare complete comet | com |

Complete these sentences. Use the words in the box.

1 Joe Kerr is a marvellous T.V. _ _ _ _c.
2 When are you going to _ _ _ _ _ _t_ that model?
3 He learned unarmed _ _ _ _ _t in the Army.
4 You can't _ _ _ _ _r_ John's work to Peter's.
5 We've had another _ _ _ _l_ _ _ _ about the noise.
6 We see Halley's _ _ _e_ every 75 years.
7 Keith hopes to _ _ _p_ _ _ in the Olympics.
8 Every school should have a micro _ _ _ _u_ _ _.

enclose antelope envelope repose	ose
grope expose slope propose	and
	ope

Complete these words by putting either **ose**
or **ope** *at the end of them. Use the words in the box.*

1 gr_ _ _   5 rep_ _ _
2 encl_ _ _   6 prop_ _ _
3 exp_ _ _   7 sl_ _ _
4 antel_ _ _   8 envel_ _ _

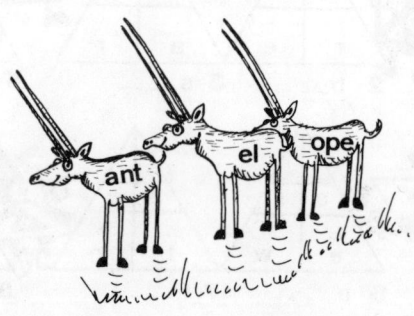

decrease defeat decimal decide detect describe detail defend defer detour	

Solve these clues. Use the words in the box.

1. a kind of fraction   (medcial)
2. to protect something   (dedfen)
3. to put off to another time   (fdeer)
4. to follow an alternative route, for example, if a road is blocked   (urtdoe)
5. to be beaten is to suffer a ?   (eatdfe)
6. to explain what something looks like   (rbeidcse)
7. to make up one's mind   (dedcie)
8. to find out by careful investigation   (etdcte)
9. what you inspect if you look at something closely   (tielad)
10. to get less or smaller   (secdreae)

project proverb provide protect produce protest profit promise progress property	

Crack this code and write out the words correctly.
They all begin with **pro.**

1. fitpro
2. gresspro
3. testpro
4. videpro
5. verbpro
6. tectpro
7. ducepro
8. jectpro
9. pertypro
10. misepro

Test 2

Complete these sentences. Each dash stands for a letter.

1 The pod opened to e _ _ _ _ _ the seeds inside.

2 The Customs officer asked, "Anything to d _ _ _ _ _ _?"

3 All was quiet then s _ _ _ _ _ _ _ a bomb exploded.

4 The submarine disappeared below the s _ _ _ _ _ _.

5 Ricky Storm is Amy's f _ _ _ _ _ _ _ _ pop singer.

6 Your work is good but could be b _ _ _ _ _.

7 Put in the letter and seal the e _ _ _ _ _ _ _.

8 Don't be vague in your answers, be d _ _ _ _ _ _ _.

9 Take care and b _ _ _ _ _ of the bull.

10 Dad likes to read my 'Beano' c _ _ _ _.

11 The bag was slung over her left s _ _ _ _ _ _ _.

12 0.5 is a d _ _ _ _ _ _ fraction.

13 This is a very i _ _ _ _ _ _ _ _ _ _ book I'm reading.

14 Brazil suffered a surprise d _ _ _ _ _ in the World Cup.

15 Your bicycle t _ _ _ has a puncture.

16 "More haste, less speed" is a good p _ _ _ _ _ _ _.

17 On the c _ _ _ _ _ _ "Go", start running on the spot.

18 You are unfit and must take more e _ _ _ _ _ _ _.

19 I c _ _ _ _ _ _ Japanese stamps.

20 We ran a program through the micro c _ _ _ _ _ _ _ _.

| refuse remark respect recall |
| resolve regret repair redundant |

Complete these sentences. Use the words in the box.

1 It is impossible to rep___ your cycle.
2 The control tower had to rec___ the aircraft.
3 Dad was made red_____ last week.
4 On January 1st you must res____ to be tidier.
5 Sorry, I must ref___ permission.
6 He asked the speaker to repeat his last rem___.
7 It is better to res____ Mr Beak than to fear him.
8 We reg___ we cannot supply books by post.

| horror terror mirror error |

Crack the code and write the words out correctly.
They all end in **rror.** *Use the words in the box.*
To help you:

e => h=< i=☐ m=∧ o=↑ t= $

rror=⌒

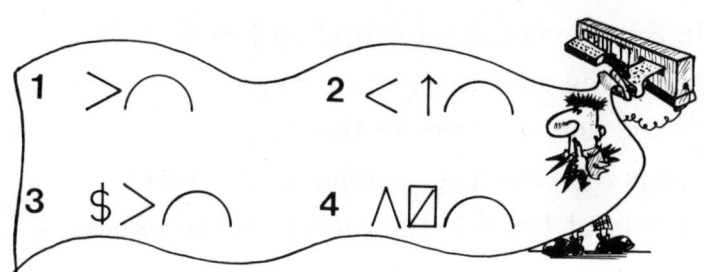

1 > ⌒   2 < ↑ ⌒

3 $ > ⌒   4 ∧ ☐ ⌒

To make the **superlative** of an
adjective which ends in **y**, drop the **y**
and add **iest**.
Examples: tiny = tiniest   merry = merriest

**funniest easiest nastiest silliest
heaviest laziest happiest prettiest**

Complete these sentences. Use the words in the box.

1 Mr Beak is h _ _ _ _ _ _ _ when Wilfred is away.
2 Wilfred is the s _ _ _ _ _ _ _ boy he has ever known.
3 He does no work so he is the l _ _ _ _ _ _ too.
4 Mr Beak's e _ _ _ _ _ _ days are when Wilfred is
   away.
5 Mr Beak's jokes are the f _ _ _ _ _ _ _.
6 Miss Fitt is the p _ _ _ _ _ _ _ _ teacher in the
   school.
7 Mr Grimm is the n _ _ _ _ _ _ _ headmaster of all.
8 Kevin, at 80 kg is the h _ _ _ _ _ _ boy in the
   school.

*Make the **ordinary** adjectives into **superlative**
adjectives in these sentences.*

1 Kevin Snudge is the (greedy) boy I know.
2 Wilfred is the (cheeky) boy in school.
3 That's the (lovely) dress in the shop.
4 Ahmed is the (wealthy) person in the world.
5 The family at No. 6 is the (noisy) in the street.
6 Bert is the (ugly) man I know.

Rule

Changing adjectives to adverbs.

Many adjectives which end in **y** drop the **y** and
add **ily**.

Examples: merry = merrily

angry = angrily

*Change these adjectives to adverbs. Remember, drop
the **y** and add **ily**.*

1	easy	4	hasty	7	speedy
2	happy	5	lucky	8	greedy
3	lazy	6	busy		

Many adjectives ending in **le** drop the **e** and add **y**.
Example: simple = simply
*Change these adjectives to adverbs. Remember, drop
the **e** and add **y**.*

1	terrible	4	possible	7	probable
2	horrible	5	sensible	8	suitable
3	reliable	6	idle		

Many adjectives ending in **e** just add **ly**.
Example: sincere = sincerely

1	delicate	4	fortunate	7	bare
2	rare	5	definite	8	vague
3	rude	6	strange		

conversation   invitation
invention   action   direction
dictionary   fraction   position

*Use the words in the box to solve the clues. Copy out
the totem pole and write in the words.*

Down

1   A talk with another person

Across

2   Where a thing is placed

3   A new idea

4   Part of a whole

5   Doing something

6   Look in this book for spellings and meanings

7   The way to go

8   You get one to go to a party

1   c
2   p _ _ _ _ _ _ n
    n
3   i _ v _ _ _ _ _ n
    _
4   f r _ _ _ _ _ n
    _
5   a _ _ _ _ n
6   d _ _ t _ _ _ _ y
7   d _ _ _ _ _ _ _ n
    o
8   i n _ _ _ _ _ _ _ n

Pause for Thought

pages 21 to 24

repair	angrily	easiest	nastiest	barely
regret	remark	reliably	invitation	
merrily	direction	happiest	hastily	recall
conversation	definitely	invention	dictionary	

Complete these sentences. Use the words in the box.

1 The Christmas bells rang m_____.

2 Look up the meaning in a d_____.

3 We are r_____ informed that the baby is a boy.

4 Peter is h_____ when playing football.

5 Gran has b_____ enough money to make ends meet.

6 Please repeat that last r_____.

7 Kevin is d_____ the best person to be captain.

8 This exercise is the e_____ one in the book.

9 We expressed our r_____ that Smith was ill.

10 I rang Amy and we had a long c_____.

11 The hovercraft is a marvellous i_____.

12 I asked the cobbler to r_____ my shoe.

13 The wind is from a northerly d_____.

14 Do the job carefully and not h_____.

15 Elton has received an i_____ to join the band.

16 Do you r_____ that holiday in Wales?

17 The furious man replied a_____ to the officer.

18 You're the meanest, n_____ person I know.

| history factory memory victory |  |

Complete these sentences. Use the words in the box.

1 Grandad has an amazing m _ _ _ _ _.
2 Trafalgar was a great v _ _ _ _ _ _ for Nelson.
3 Wilfred can't remember dates in h _ _ _ _ _ _.
4 Uncle Sid works at the glue f _ _ _ _ _ _.

| forty idly magazine machine |  |

Complete these sentences. Use the words in the box.

1 Mum's washing m _ _ _ _ _ _ is broken.
2 Tom is f _ _ _ _ years of age.
3 Mum buys a m _ _ _ _ _ _ _ every week.
4 People stood i _ _ _ by, watching the fire.

| discovery disgusted distant disappear disobey disapprove discuss disappointed |  |

Complete these words by adding **dis.**

1 _ _ _approve
2 _ _ _appear
3 _ _ _covery
4 _ _ _cuss
5 _ _ _obey
6 _ _ _gusted
7 _ _ _tant
8 _ _ _appointed

26

salary February ordinary missionary January library canary boundary	

Complete these sentences. Use the words in the box.

1 I make a resolution every J _ _ _ _ _ _ 1st.

2 Take these books back to the l _ _ _ _ _ _ for me.

3 This c _ _ _ _ _ sings loudly.

4 The batsman scored a b _ _ _ _ _ _ _ from every ball.

5 Livingstone was an explorer and a m _ _ _ _ _ _ _ _ _.

6 My father's s _ _ _ _ _ is paid monthly.

7 The month before March is F _ _ _ _ _ _ _.

8 She isn't special, just an o _ _ _ _ _ _ _ girl.

remedy fury beauty busy duty truly study deny	

Computer fault printout ⬜ *instead of* **y**. *Correct these words. Use the words in the box.*

1 den ⬜

2 stud ⬜

3 trul ⬜

4 dut ⬜

5 bus ⬜

6 beaut ⬜

7 fur ⬜

8 remed ⬜

rattle	struggle	idle	bottle	battle
settle	riddle	puzzle	cattle	shuffle

le

Crack this code and write the words out correctly.
All the words end with the same two letters.
To help you: a = B   b = C   c = D
Example: UJDLMF = tickle

1 TFUUMF
2 TUSVHHMF
3 TIVGGMF
4 CPUUMF
5 QVAAMF

6 JEMF
7 CBUUMF
8 DBUUMF
9 SBUUMF
10 SJEEMF

---

rifle scribble tremble noble
invisible possible sensible stumble

Complete these sentences. Use the words in the box.

1 The n _ _ _ _ lord gave food to the peasants.
2 Ian began to shiver and t _ _ _ _ _ _.
3 I saw her s _ _ _ _ _ _ and fall downstairs.
4 Go home to bed as soon as p _ _ _ _ _ _ _.
5 If you can't see it, it's i _ _ _ _ _ _ _ _.
6 Everybody was s _ _ _ _ _ _ _, refusing to panic.
7 The toddler began to s _ _ _ _ _ _ _ on the wall.
8 The soldier fired his r _ _ _ _.

argument	measurement	excitement	
treatment	advertisement	instrument	
ornament	punishment		

Work out these mixed up words. They all end in
ment. *Use the words in the box.*

1 tann more   3 en rag tum
2 amen sure met   4 at rem tent

Complete these sentences. Use the words in the box.

1 The naughty boy deserves his p_____.
2 You can feel the e_____ in the air!
3 The guitar is a pleasant i_____.
4 I saw an a_____ in the newspaper.

| enjoyment   annoy   destroy   employ |

Complete these sentences. Use the words in the box.

1 A nuclear bomb would d_____ London.
2 We hope to e_____ fifty men at the factory.
3 Music gives people great e_____.
4 Wilfred does silly things that a____ Mr Beak.

29

Test 3

pages 21 to 29

Complete these sentences. Each dash stands for a letter.

1 The b _ _ _ _ _ of milk is nearly empty.

2 We watched the genie d _ _ _ _ _ _ _ _ before our eyes.

3 The shortest month is F _ _ _ _ _ _ _.

4 If you d _ _ _ _ _ _ Mr Beak, you'll be punished.

5 Someone must r _ _ _ _ _ that broken T.V.

6 'New Musical Express' is a m _ _ _ _ _ _ _ for pop fans.

7 Mollie is the p _ _ _ _ _ _ _ _ girl in the village.

8 Grandad has a very good m _ _ _ _ _.

9 Films about Dracula are h _ _ _ _ _ films.

10 Coco's the f _ _ _ _ _ _ _ clown I've ever seen.

11 I dropped the key, but l _ _ _ _ _ _ I found it again.

12 The m _ _ _ _ _ _ _ _ _ taught the cannibals about God.

13 I will always r _ _ _ _ _ not saving more money.

14 There are thousands of books in the l _ _ _ _ _ _ _.

15 The bees were b _ _ _ _ _ collecting honey.

16 Seven years' bad luck if you break a m _ _ _ _ _!

17 Another word for a cure is a r _ _ _ _ _.

18 Professor Branestawm showed off his i _ _ _ _ _ _ _ _.

19 The opposite of accept is r _ _ _ _ _.

20 What you did was a very hasty a _ _ _ _ _.

exercise	expense	except	exact
exclaim	explain	exceed	excuse

*These words start with **eggs** instead of **ex**. Write the words out correctly. Use the words in the box.*

1 eggsplain   5 eggscept

2 eggscuse   6 eggsclaim

3 eggsact   7 eggspense

4 eggsceed   8 eggsercise

excuse	experiment	explosive
expand	expert	exchange

*Answer the clues. All the words begin with **ex**.*
Write out the words correctly.

1 To become bigger

2 This is put into bombs and shells

3 Someone who knows all about a subject

4 What you might give to your teacher when you are late

5 To prove something, you try an e _ _ _ _ _ _ _ _.

6 To swap something

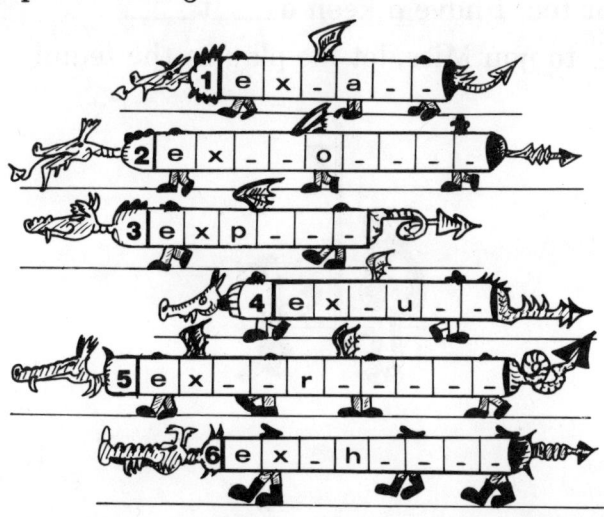

31

| accounted | accused | account | accident |
| accelerate | accept | accompany | accurate |

Complete these sentences. Use the words in the box.

1 You are a__u___ of stealing £1000.
2 You must a__o___ for every penny you spend.
3 Kindly a____p___ me to the police station.
4 My new watch is a_____t_ to the second.
5 We have a_____d for everyone on the coach.
6 We heard the car a____e____ away at high speed.
7 Please a____t our apologies for the mix-up.
8 The ambulance was called to an a___d___.

| appeal | appoint | appetite |
| applaud | approve | |

Complete these sentences. Use the words in the box.

1 Listen to the crowd as they a__l___ their team!
2 Miss Print does not a__r___ of punk hair styles.
3 We shall a__o___ Mr Trodd as Headmaster.
4 What's for tea, I have a keen a___t___.
5 I a__e__ to you Miss, let me play in the team!

> **value statue rescue queue**
> **glue continue clue avenue**

Complete these sentences. Use the words in the box.

1 That g _ _ _ will never stick wood.
2 Holmes said, "I have found a c _ _ _ !"
3 I'll c _ _ _ _ _ _ _ reading the story tomorrow.
4 A long q _ _ _ _ formed outside the shop.
5 The lifeboat managed to r _ _ _ _ _ the crew.
6 A s _ _ _ _ _ of the Mayor stands in the square.
7 That ornament is of little v _ _ _ _ to anyone.
8 We drove through a long a _ _ _ _ _ of trees.

> **induce reduce introduce**
> **deduce produce spruce**

Crack this code and write out the words correctly.
*They all end in **uce**. Use the words in the box*
to help you.

Example: ecup = puce

1 ecudortni   4 ecuder
2 ecudorp   5 ecudni
3 ecuded   6 ecurps

wealth	width	fifth	strength	ninth
length	warmth	seventh	depth	growth

Answer these clues. Use the words in the box.
All the words end in **th.**

1 Area of a rectangle = width × l_ _ _ _ _ _.
2 As a plant develops you can watch its g _ _ _ _ _ _.
3 You need s _ _ _ _ _ _ _ to be a weight-lifter.
4 Three is one n _ _ _ _ of twenty seven.
5 Great riches are called w _ _ _ _ _.
6 You get w _ _ _ _ _ from a fire or radiator.
7 Area of a rectangle = length × w _ _ _ _.
8 Third, fourth, f _ _ _ _, sixth.
9 From the surface to the sea-bed is the d _ _ _ _ of the sea.
10 Five is one s _ _ _ _ _ _ of thirty five.

---

thirteen	sixth	twelfth	seventh

Complete these sentences. Use the words in the box.
Copy out the wall and fill it in.

1 Four is one _ _ _ _ _ of 24.
2 Seven is one _ _ _ _ _ _ _ of 49.
3 Twelve is one _ _ _ _ _ _ _ of 144.
4 Unlucky for some ?

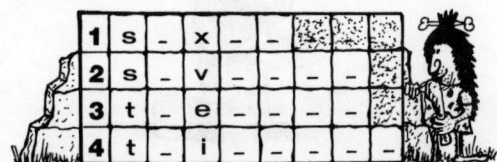

Pause for Thought

pages 31 to 34

introduce	applaud	length	experiment	approve
value	exchange	accurate	warmth	accelerate
strength	queue	expand	exercise	expert
exciting	rescue	appeal	continue	reduce

Complete these sentences. Use the words in the box.

1   We will c _____ this enquiry tomorrow.
2   Everyone should take regular e _____.
3   The balloon began to e _____, swelling rapidly.
4   A long q ____ waited for the bus.
5   Joe pulled at the rope with all his s _____.
6   Suddenly the car began to a _____.
7   Add it up and be as a _____ as possible.
8   The audience began to a _____ the choir.
9   Will you i _____ me to your sister?
10   Take it back and ask the shop to e _____ it.
11   The shop will r _____ its prices in the sale.
12   The condemned man made an a _____ for mercy.
13   The talk about Africa will be given by an e _____.
14   The puppies huddled together for w _____.
15   I hope you will a _____ of my purchases.
16   Prove the theory by doing an e _____.
17   A helicopter was used to r _____ the survivors.
18   Your jewellery is of little v ____.
19   Measure the width and l _____ of the room.
20   The cup final should be an e _____ game.

> **luggage damage bandage postage
> village message manage advantage**
>
> **age**

Complete these sentences. Use the words in the box.

1 Take James to the sickroom and b _ _ _ _ _ _ the cut.

2 There is no a _ _ _ _ _ _ _ _ in arriving early.

3 This letter needs 25p p _ _ _ _ _ _.

4 Take a m _ _ _ _ _ _ to Miss Take for me.

5 Help me to put the l _ _ _ _ _ _ in the car.

6 In the middle of the v _ _ _ _ _ _ is a duck pond.

7 Take care, you mustn't d _ _ _ _ _ that vase.

8 Can you m _ _ _ _ _ to sleep with all the noise?

> **bright right delight plight
> tight fright flight sight**
>
> **ight**

Crack the code and write the words out correctly.
Use the words in the box.
To help you: a = B   b = C   c = D   and z = A

1 TJHIU

2 EFMJHIU

3 GSJHIU

4 CSJHIU

5 UJHIU

6 SJHIU

7 GMJHIU

8 QMJHIU

chemist chord choir echo ache	

Complete these sentences. Use the words in the box.

1   Kevin had an audition for the church c _ _ _ _.
2   Go to the c _ _ _ _ _ _ and buy some aspirin.
3   My feet hurt and my legs a _ _ _.
4   Can you play a c _ _ _ _ on your guitar?
5   Hans yodelled and the e _ _ _ came back.

demand depress detail depend dessert	

Complete these sentences. Use the words in the box.

1   Another name for a pudding is a des _ _ _ _.
2   You can dep _ _ _ on Mick to do a good job.
3   Her description was correct in every det _ _ _.
4   I will write and dem _ _ _ a refund.
5   Oh dear, this rainy weather does dep _ _ _ _ me!

rhymes rhubarb rhinoceros rhythm	

Complete the sentences. Use the words in the box.

1   The drums beat out a regular rhy _ _ _.
2   My little sister likes nursery rhy _ _ _.
3   Mum is going to make a rhu _ _ _ _ pie.
4   The rhi _ _ _ _ _ _ _ is a dangerous animal.

knitted knuckles
knee knowledge

silent k

Complete these sentences. Use the words in the box.

1 Who k _ _ _ _ _ _ that lovely sweater for you?
2 Some people get all their k _ _ _ _ _ _ _ _ from books.
3 Jenny fell and grazed her k _ _ _.
4 Mark skinned his k _ _ _ _ _ _ _ climbing trees.

wrestle wrinkles wriggle wrist

silent W

Complete these sentences. Use the words in the box.

1 Do sit still Wilfred and don't w _ _ g _ _ _ so.
2 My forehead is full of w _ _ _ k _ _ _.
3 Your w _ _ s _ connects your hand to your arm.
4 You two boys must not w _ e _ _ _ _ in the kitchen.

science schedule scent

silent c

Complete these sentences. Use the words in the box.

1 The hounds have picked up the s _ _ _ t of the fox.
2 Flight 222 landed at Gatwick on sch _ _ _ _ _.
3 I like chemistry best of all the sci _ _ _ _ lessons.

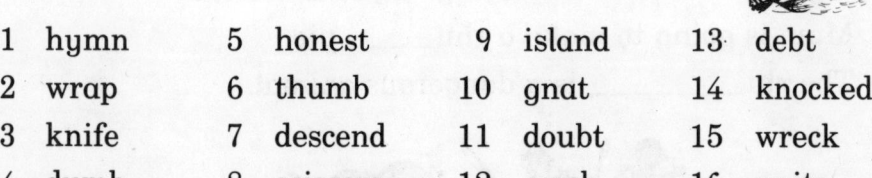

What is the silent letter in each of these words?

1 hymn	5 honest	9 island	13 debt
2 wrap	6 thumb	10 gnat	14 knocked
3 knife	7 descend	11 doubt	15 wreck
4 dumb	8 scissors	12 comb	16 write

| guard   guest   guide   guilty |
| disguise   guarantee   guitar   guess |

silent
u

Complete these sentences. Use the words in the box.

1   Eric got a shock from the electric g _ _ _ _ r.
2   The judge said Evans was g _ _ _ _ y.
3   The soldier was on g _ _ _ d all night.
4   Can you g _ _ _ s how much money I have?
5   The hunters needed a g _ _ _ e through the forest.
6   We have a French student staying as our g _ _ _ t.
7   Everyone saw through Sidney's d _ _ _ _ _ _ e.
8   This radio has a two year g _ _ _ _ _ _ _ e.

| quarter   quarry   quarrel |
| question   quiver |

qu

Complete these sentences. Use the words in the box.

1   Phil and John had a q _ _ _ _ _ l ending in a fight.
2   Slate is dug in a q _ _ _ _ y.
3   Twenty five is one q _ _ _ t _ _ of a hundred.
4   Robin had a q _ _ _ _ r full of arrows.
5   Go on, ask me another q _ _ _ _ _ _ n.

Test 4

Complete these sentences. Each dash stands for a letter.

1 We will c_ _ _ _ _ _ _ with this lesson after break.

2 Ten is one f_ _ _ _ of fifty.

3 Peter used all his s_ _ _ _ _ _ _ to break the string.

4 Ten motor-cyclists will a_ _ _ _ _ _ _ _ the Royal car.

5 The Gas Board say that the money is d_ _ now.

6 We will a_ _ _ _ _ your offer.

7 Terry has awful tooth a_ _ _.

8 I don't understand, please r_ _ _ _ _ that again.

9 You can always d_ _ _ _ _ on Dick to be late.

10 Please i_ _ _ _ _ _ _ _ me to your cousin.

11 Can you g_ _ _ _ what I am getting for Christmas?

12 Can I e_ _ _ _ _ _ _ this shirt for a bigger one?

13 Five is a q_ _ _ _ _ _ of twenty.

14 There was a long q_ _ _ _ outside the cinema.

15 Our car was damaged in an a_ _ _ _ _ _ _.

16 The old man's face was a mass of w_ _ _ _ _ _ _.

17 The police called in a handwriting e_ _ _ _ _ _.

18 The hounds picked up the s_ _ _ _ of the fox.

19 We g_ _ _ _ _ _ _ _ the bike for six months.

20 If you owe money, you are in d_ _ _.

Answer these clues. Use the words in the box. Copy out the puzzle and write in the words.

Across
1 Opposite of presence   a _ _ _ _ _ _
2 It won't move, it won't   b _ _ _ _
3 As s _ _ _ _ as the rock of Gibraltar
4 The person in charge of a trial in court   j _ _ _ _
5 On time, punctual   p _ _ _ _ _

Down
6 Silly, nonsensical, foolish   a _ _ _ _ _ _
7 The way of doing a task   m _ _ _ _ _
8 False, not real   a _ _ _ _ _ _ _ _ _
9 Opposite of full   e _ _ _ _

Complete these sentences. Use the words in the box.

1 I can't do this crossword p _ _ _ _ _.

2 Tom walked through a deep p _ _ _ _ _.

3 Hiroshima was destroyed by an a _ _ _ _ _ bomb.

4 Can I have a cheese s _ _ _ _ _ _ _, please?

5 King Trogg is ruler of a huge k _ _ _ _ _ _.

6 The policeman said Tom was over the speed
    l _ _ _ _.

7 The volcano became a _ _ _ _ _ _ after fifty years.

8 I write in my d _ _ _ _ every day.

**thigh tonight sigh tighten
high sight delighted might**

igh

*Crack this code and work out the code words in the
sentences. They are printed in capital letters.
To help you: a = B   b = C   c = D   up to z = A.*

1 I would be EFMJHIUFE if you came to stay.

2 You must UJHIUFO the straps more than that.

3 Tom NJHIU be allowed to come if he behaves.

4 The fireworks were a wonderful TJHIU.

5 Why do you TJHI like that, are you sad?

i Erroll has a bandage round his UIJHI.

   The balloon soared IJHI into the sky.

   My favourite programme is on T.V. UPOJHIU.

rr
and
ll

| pillar torrent current pillow |
| caterpillar dollar collar mirror |

Complete these sentences. Use the words in the box.

1 An electric c_____ runs through that cable.

2 One hundred cents makes a d_____.

3 She fell asleep as her head hit the p_____.

4 In minutes the stream became a raging t_____.

5 The c_____ of your shirt is torn.

6 A c_____ becomes a butterfly.

7 That p_____ supports the whole building.

8 Look at your reflection in that m_____.

el

| channel kennel tunnel parcel |
| funnel label travel |

Complete these sentences. Use the words in the box.

1 There are plans to dig a Channel t_____.

2 It is quicker to _r____ by aeroplane.

3 Water went rushing along the narrow c_____.

4 Make sure you wrap the p_____ securely.

5 Write the address on the l____ clearly.

6 Our dog lives in a k_____.

7 Use a f_____ to pour petrol into the tank.

Two Rules

all right is two words, not one.

thank you is two words, not one.

allowed protect frowned hero
drowned heroine direct remembered

assorted

Complete these sentences. Use the words in the box.

1   Mr Beak f_____ at Wilfred.
2   You are a h___ if you win the V.C.
3   Sally has just r_____ an appointment.
4   Please could you d_____ me to the station?
5   All the crew were d_____ when the ship sank.
6   You must p_____ the plants from frost.
7   No smoking is a_____ in the theatre.
8   The female equivalent of 'hero' is 'h_____'.

enough tough although bough trough
cough plough rough through dough

ough

Crack the code and work out the code words. Find out
how to say them. Use the words in the box to help you.
This is the code: a = 1   b = 2   c = 3   d = 4   up to z = 26

1   2 : 15 : 21 : 7 : 8
2   16 : 12 : 15 : 21 : 7 : 8
3   3 : 15 : 21 : 7 : 8
4   20 : 18 : 15 : 21 : 7 : 8
5   4 : 15 : 21 : 7 : 8
6   1 : 12 : 20 : 8 : 15 : 21 : 7 : 8
7   20 : 15 : 21 : 7 : 8
8   18 : 15 : 21 : 7 : 8
9   5 : 14 : 15 : 21 : 7 : 8
10   20 : 8 : 18 : 15 : 21 : 7 : 8

| elephant photograph dolphin nephew alphabet telephone sphere autograph |  |

Complete these sentences. Use the words in the box.

1 A d_____ is a very intelligent animal.
2 Uncle John has come to see his favourite n_____.
3 Answer the t_____, please.
4 An e_____ never forgets.
5 Take a p_____ with your new camera.
6 Another name for a globe or ball is a s_____.
7 There are twenty six letters in the a_____.
8 I asked the pop star for his a_____.

Some nouns ending in a **consonant** and **o** add **es** to make them plural.
Example: potato = potatoes

| tomatoes volcanoes cargoes heroes echoes |  |

*Rewrite the **singular** words in italics as **plurals**.*
Use the words in the box.

1 The ships were loaded with heavy *cargo*.
2 Tom and Harry won medals and are *hero*.
3 There are many *volcano* in Iceland.
4 I would like lettuce and *tomato* in my salad.
5 We shouted and listened to the *echo*.

Complete these sentences. Use the words in the box.

1   Nelson won a famous v _ _ _ _ _ _ at Trafalgar.

2   Joe s _ _ _ _ _ comes to meetings nowadays.

3   Sixteen plus three makes n _ _ _ _ _ _ _ _.

4   Aim for the bull's eye in the c _ _ _ _ _ of the target.

5   Pay your bill promptly and get a 20% d _ _ _ _ _ _ _ _.

6   We should s _ _ _ _ _ Erroll for the football team.

7   The ghost made its a _ _ _ _ _ _ _ _ _ at midnight.

8   Two sevens make f _ _ _ _ _ _ _.

---

noticeable valuable comfortable	
reliable terrible sensible	**able**
horrible probable possible	*and*
available movable visible	**ible**

*When decoded, seven of these words end in **able** and five of them end in **ible**. Crack the code and write out the words correctly. The words in the box will help you.*

1   elbavom

2   elbaulav

3   elbirret

4   elbissop

5   elbaliava

6   elbaborp

7   elbatrofmoc

8   elbisiv

9   elbisnes

10   elbaeciton

11   elbirroh

12   elbailer

Pause for Thought

hero receiver absurd current supply reply discount artificial direct alphabet sandwich rely caterpillar appearance parcel nephew photograph kingdom dollar elephant

Complete these sentences. Use the words in the box.

1 You can r_ _ _ on Jim to tell a good story.

2 Buy real flowers; I hate a_ _ _ _ _ _ _ _ ones.

3 Amy is my niece and her brother is my n_ _ _ _ _.

4 We give you a 5% d_ _ _ _ _ _ _ for paying in cash.

5 The Queen is ruler of this k_ _ _ _ _ _.

6 The actor made a personal a_ _ _ _ _ _ _ _ _.

7 The a_ _ _ _ _ _ _ begins with the letters a,b,c.

8 I'd rather be a live coward than a dead h_ _ _.

9 The d_ _ _ _ _ is a unit of American money.

10 The c_ _ _ _ _ _ in the river is very fast.

11 Our telephone r_ _ _ _ _ _ _ is white.

12 The biggest land animal is the e_ _ _ _ _ _ _.

13 The 17.40 train goes d_ _ _ _ _ to London.

14 It is rude of you not to r_ _ _ _ to his letter.

15 Tie that string tightly around the p_ _ _ _ _.

16 That c_ _ _ _ _ _ _ _ _ _ will soon become a cocoon.

17 The new firm can s_ _ _ _ _ all your needs.

18 Can I have a peanut butter s_ _ _ _ _ _ _, please?

19 You will need a p_ _ _ _ _ _ _ _ _ on your passport.

20 What, fly in that thing, don't be a_ _ _ _ _!

Maxi Test for YOU

Complete these sentences. Each dash stands for a letter.

1   There was a short i _ _ _ _ _ _ _ between films.

2   Be c _ _ _ _ _ _ when you handle the eggs.

3   The plane dived out of c _ _ _ _ _ _.

4   That horse is the certain w _ _ _ _ _ of the Derby.

5   You can have roast or b _ _ _ _ _ potatoes.

6   Sitting Bull was c _ _ _ _ of the Sioux tribe.

7   Wilfred stuck a pin in the b _ _ _ _ _ _ and burst it.

8   We will soon be living in the 21st c _ _ _ _ _ _.

9   Stick down the e _ _ _ _ _ _ _ and post the letter.

10   Yes, I am sure, that is d _ _ _ _ _ _ _ _ _ the man.

11   If you never lied we could b _ _ _ _ _ _ you now.

12   It is not p _ _ _ _ _ _ _ for men to live on Mercury.

13   Now d _ _ _ _ _ _ _ the thief's clothing for me.

14   The attempt to wreck the train was
       d _ _ _ _ _ _ _ _ _.

15   Emma's favourite c _ _ _ _ is the 'Beano'.

16   Do it again and correct every e _ _ _ _.

17   Run the program on the c _ _ _ _ _ _ _.

18   A serious a _ _ _ _ _ _ _ occurred on the motorway.

19   This radio must go to the shop for r _ _ _ _ _.

20   The flashing light was obviously a s _ _ _ _ _ _.

21   Passengers were c _ _ _ _ _ _ _ their own luggage.

22   I saw the submarine as it came to the s _ _ _ _ _ _.

23   Get me another book from the l _ _ _ _ _ _, please.

24   We l _ _ _ _ _ _ _ to the news on the radio.

25   Try to g _ _ _ _ how old I am.